# SING TOGETHER!

## ALPHABETICAL LIST OF CONTENTS
*(First lines in italics)*

| | No. | | No. |
|---|---|---|---|
| *A good sword and a trusty hand!* | 85 | Faithful Johnny | 58 |
| *A little man is standing within the wood* | 9 | Farewell, Manchester! | 57 |
| *A north-country maid* | 86 | Farmyard, The | 27 |
| *A shepherdess was watching* | 30 | Fire Down Below | 26 |
| *A sly old fox am I* | 14 | *Fire in the galley* | 26 |
| Afton Water | 69 | Fisherman's Night Song | 56 |
| *All in a wood there grew a tree* | 73 | Flight of the Earls, The | 96 |
| Andulko | 28 | *Flow gently, sweet Afton* | 69 |
| Animals went in Two by Two, The | 39 | Fox's Song, The | 14 |
| Anna Marie | 15 | | |
| *Around Cape Horn we're bound to go* | 41 | Gay Musician, The | 13 |
| A-roving | 71 | Golden Slumbers | 72 |
| *As I sat on the hillside* | 6 | Green and White | 10 |
| *As pretty Polly Oliver lay musing in bed* | 47 | *Green, green, green's the colour* | 10 |
| Ash Grove, The | 70 | Green grow the Leaves | 36 |
| | | Green grow the Rushes, ho! | 74 |
| Barbara Allen | 65 | | |
| Barnyard Song, The | 34 | *Hark! I hear the foe advancing* | 91 |
| Bay of Biscay, The | 100 | Heart of Oak | 95 |
| Blow away the Morning Dew | 68 | *Hey, jim along* | 5 |
| Bobby Shafto | 32 | High Germany | 94 |
| Boney was a Warrior | 22 | Ho-la-hi | 55 |
| *Bonnie Charlie's noo awa* | 81 | Hope, the Hermit | 54 |
| Bonnie Dundee | 99 | | |
| *Bring the good old bugle, boys* | 75 | *I am a gay musician* | 13 |
| British Grenadiers, The | 63 | *I came from Alabama* | 37 |
| *By yon bonnie banks* | 93 | *I cobble, cobble all day long* | 8 |
| | | *I had a cat and the cat pleased me* | 34 |
| Cader Idris | 67 | *I know a gal that you don't know* | 40 |
| Camptown Races | 78 | *I thought I heard the skipper say* | 46 |
| Captain Morgan's March | 61 | *I'll sing you one-ho!* | 74 |
| Charlie is my Darling | 66 | *In Amsterdam there lived a maid* | 71 |
| Cobbler and the Crow, The | 33 | *In Dublin's fair city* | 64 |
| Cockles and Mussels | 64 | *In good King Charles's golden days* | 84 |
| *Come, cheer up, my lads* | 95 | *In Scarlet Town, where I was born* | 65 |
| Come Home Now | 12 | *In the calm hour of evening* | 56 |
| Cuckoo, The | 62 | I'se the B'y that builds the Boat | 52 |
| | | *I've been to Harlem, I've been to Dover* | 35 |
| Darby Kelly | 98 | | |
| *Do you ken Elsie Marley, honey?* | 59 | Jennie Jenkins | 77 |
| Donkey Riding | 24 | Jim along Josie | 5 |
| Down in Demerara | 23 | John Barleycorn | 53 |
| *Down yonder green valley* | 70 | John Brown's Body | 76 |
| Drink to me Only | 97 | John Smith, Fellow Fine | 11 |
| | | | |
| Early One Morning | 60 | Keeper, The | 18 |
| Elsie Marley | 59 | | |

## ALPHABETICAL LIST OF CONTENTS

| | No. |
|---|---|
| Lass of Richmond Hill, The | 50 |
| *Lazy sheep, pray tell me why* | 31 |
| Leave her, Johnny | 46 |
| *Lighthearted I stroll through the Vale* | 67 |
| Li'l Liza Jane | 40 |
| Lincolnshire Poacher, The | 51 |
| *Listen to the cheerful cry* | 55 |
| Little Boy and the Sheep, The | 31 |
| Loch Lomond | 93 |
| "Look, who comes here!" | 7 |
| *Lou, Lou, skip to my Lou* | 4 |
| *Loud roars the dreadful thunder* | 100 |
| | |
| Mallow Fling, The | 92 |
| Marching through Georgia | 75 |
| Men of Harlech | 91 |
| *Men of Morganwg, rise against the foe!* | 61 |
| Mermaid, The | 90 |
| Merry Cobbler, The | 8 |
| Michael Finnigin | 16 |
| Miller of Dee, The | 89 |
| Minstrel Boy, The | 88 |
| My Aunt Jemima | 3 |
| My Bonny Cuckoo | 87 |
| My Father's Garden | 2 |
| *My grandsire beat the drum complete* | 98 |
| *My sweetheart, come along* | 45 |
| | |
| Noble Duke of York, The | 1 |
| *Now I'm going to sing to you* | 3 |
| *Now the sun is shining brightly* | 92 |
| | |
| *O Polly, love, O Polly* | 94 |
| O Rare Turpin | 49 |
| *O Shenandoah, I long to hear you* | 38 |
| *O will you wear white, O my dear* | 77 |
| Oak and the Ash, The | 86 |
| *Oh, I went to Peter's flowing spring* | 62 |
| Oh, Susanna | 37 |
| *Oh, the noble Duke of York* | 1 |
| *Oh, where are you going, my Anna Marie?* | 15 |
| *Oh, where are you going, my pretty maid?* | 44 |
| *On Hounslow Heath as I rode o'er* | 49 |
| *On Richmond Hill there lives a lass* | 50 |
| *Once a jolly swagman* | 83 |
| *Once in a blithe greenwood* | 54 |
| *One Friday morn when we set sail* | 90 |
| One Man went to Mow | 20 |
| | |
| Pretty Polly Oliver | 47 |
| Punchinello | 7 |

| | No. |
|---|---|
| Riddle, The | 9 |
| Rio Grande | 44 |
| Robin Adair | 48 |
| | |
| Sacramento | 41 |
| Sally Brown | 42 |
| Scraping up Sand | 29 |
| *See at the water's edge* | 43 |
| Shenandoah | 38 |
| Shepherdess, The | 30 |
| Skip to my Lou | 4 |
| Smuggler's Song, The | 43 |
| *Some talk of Alexander* | 63 |
| Song of the Western Men | 85 |
| Spring Song | 6 |
| Sweet Nightingale | 45 |
| | |
| Ten in the Bed | 19 |
| *The Camptown ladies sing this song* | 78 |
| *There came three men* | 53 |
| There was a Jolly Miller | 21 |
| *There was a jolly miller once* | 89 |
| *There was a man who had a horselum* | 23 |
| *There was a merry cobbler* | 33 |
| *There was an old man* | 16 |
| *There were ten in the bed* | 19 |
| This Old Man | 17 |
| *Three gipsies stood at the castle gate* | 80 |
| *To other shores across the sea* | 96 |
| *To the Lords of Convention* | 99 |
| Tree in the Wood, The | 73 |
| Turn the Glasses Over | 35 |
| | |
| *Up was I on my father's farm* | 27 |
| *Upon the sweetest summertime* | 68 |
| | |
| Vicar of Bray, The | 84 |
| | |
| Waltzing Matilda | 83 |
| We be Three Poor Mariners | 82 |
| *Were you ever in Quebec?* | 24 |
| What shall we do with the Drunken Sailor? | 25 |
| *What's this dull town to me?* | 48 |
| *When I was bound apprentice* | 51 |
| *When will you come again?* | 58 |
| Will Ye no Come Back Again? | 81 |
| Wraggle Taggle Gipsies, The | 80 |
| | |
| Ye Banks and Braes | 79 |

# I. THE NOBLE DUKE OF YORK

English traditional song

Oh, the no-ble Duke of York, He had ten thou-sand men, He marched them up to the top of the hill And he marched them down a - gain.

1. And when they were up they were up, And when they were down they were down, And when they were on - ly half way up They were neith - er up nor down.
2. They look'd all a - round and a - round, But noth - ing at all could they find, Ex - cept a big hay-stack in a field, And that they left be - hind.
3. The Eng - lish-man said, "Tis a stack," The Scots - man he said, "Nay," The I - rish-man said it was a church With the stee - ple blown a - way.

Oh, the

Printed in Great Britain
OXFORD UNIVERSITY PRESS, MUSIC DEPARTMENT, GREAT CLARENDON STREET, OXFORD OX2 6DP

# 2. MY FATHER'S GARDEN

French traditional song, with words by Frederick Fowler

1.&2. My fa - ther has a gar - den With

ma - ny li - lac trees, _____ My fa - ther has a

gar - den With ma - ny li - lac trees, _____ (1.) With / (2.) With

branch - es spread - ing sky - wards And sway - ing in the breeze._
branch - es for the birds' nests And flow - ers for the bees._

Come in - to our gar - den, come and see the li - lacs there,

Come in - to our gar - den, li - lacs ev - 'ry - where!_

3

# 3. MY AUNT JEMIMA

Traditional German tune

Now I'm going to sing to you
'Bout my Aunt Je - mi - ma. She made plas-ter of the best
Down in Ca - ro - li - na. Sheep-skin and the bees' good wax,
Thun-der- pitch for plas - ter: If you try to pull it off,
It will stick the fas - ter. Skin a ma, lick ma,
doo - dle di, Skin a ma, lick ma di - do.

Skin a ma, lick ma, doo- dle di, Skin a ma, lick ma di - do.

4

# 4. SKIP TO MY LOU

American folk-song

Lou, Lou, skip to my Lou;
Lou, Lou, skip to my Lou; Lou, Lou,
skip to my Lou; Skip to my Lou, my dar - ling.

1. Lost my part - ner, what'll I do? Lost my part - ner,
2. I'll find a-nother one pretty as you, I'll find a-nother one

what'll I do? Lost my part - ner,
pretty as you, I'll find a-nother one

what'll I do? Skip to my Lou, my dar - ling.
pretty as you, Skip to my Lou, my dar - ling.

3 Cows in the meadow, Moo, Moo, Moo!

4 Flies in the sugar bowl, Shoo, Shoo, Shoo!

# 5. JIM ALONG JOSIE

American folk-song

1. Hey, jim a - long,— jim a - long Jo - sie,
2. Walk jim a - long,— jim a - long Jo - sie,

Hey, jim a - long,— jim a - long Jo.
Walk jim a - long,— jim a - long Jo.

Hey, jim a - long,—
Walk jim a - long,—

jim a - long Jo - sie, Hey, jim a - long,— jim a - long Jo.
jim a - long Jo - sie, Walk jim a - long,— jim a - long Jo.

| 3 | Hop jim along | 5 | Jump jim along | 7 | Swing jim along |
| 4 | Run jim along | 6 | Crawl jim along | 8 | Roll jim along |

Jim along = jog along

# 6. SPRING SONG

German folk-song; English version by Frances B. Wood

1. As I sat on the— hill - side I—
2. As I walked in the— gar - den Bees—

heard the birds— sing, And I watched them a -
buzzed a - way— home, With their sweet load of—

-build - ing Their— nests in the Spring.
hon - ey To — store in the comb.

6

# 7. PUNCHINELLO

French folk-song; English version by Frances B. Wood

1. "Look, who comes here! Why it's
2. "Play for us now; we are

Mis - ter Punch - i - nel - lo. Look! Punch and
read - y, Punch - i - nel - lo. Play for us

Ju - dy are back a - gain to town.
now; we all love to watch your fun."

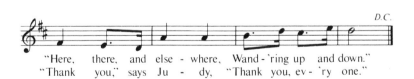

Where have you been?— We've missed you, Punch-i - nel - lo."
Round comes the hat— and in we pop our pen - nies.

*D.C.*

"Here, there, and else - where, Wand - 'ring up and down."
"Thank you," says Ju - dy, "Thank you, ev - 'ry one."

# 8. THE MERRY COBBLER

Belgian folk-song; English version by Frances B. Wood

1. I cob-ble, cob-ble all day long |
2. With tap, tap, tap, I heel and sole: |

Tra, la-de-dee - ra. And, as I work, I sing this song. |
With stitch, stitch, stitch, I make shoes whole. |

Tra, la - de - fal - de - dee, Tra, la - de - dee - ra.

3   Just send your boots and shoes to me,
    No matter how worn out they be.

4   Then back they'll come as good as new.
    Yes, I'm the cobbler man for you.

# 9. THE RIDDLE

German folk-song, translated by Elizabeth Fiske

1. A lit - tle man is
2. The lit - tle man is

stand - ing with - in the wood; He wears a pur - ple
si - lent and makes no sound; He stands with on - ly

8

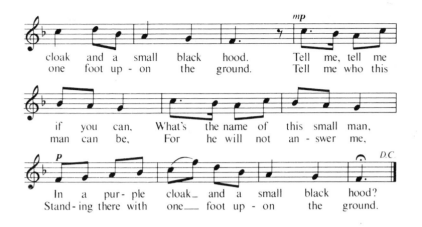

cloak and a small black hood. Tell me, tell me
one foot up - on the ground. Tell me who this

if you can, What's the name of this small man,
man can be, For he will not an - swer me,

In a pur - ple cloak__ and a small black hood?
Stand - ing there with one__ foot up - on the ground.

## 10. GREEN AND WHITE

German folk-song, translated by John Horton

1. Green, green, green's the co - lour of my
2. White, white, white's the co - lour of my

gar - ments, Green, green, green my on - ly wear shall be.
gar - ments, White, white, white my on - ly wear shall be.

If you'd have me tell you why I love it
If you'd have me tell you why I love it

dear - ly: My true love a game-keep - er is he!
dear - ly: My true love a ba - ker's man is he!

## 11. JOHN SMITH, FELLOW FINE

Scottish folk-song

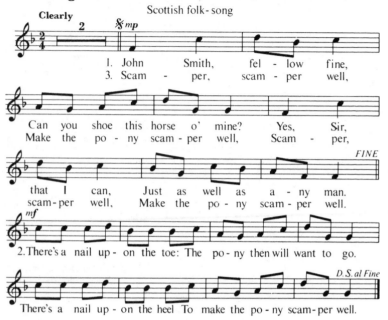

Clearly

1. John Smith, fel - low fine,
3. Scam - per, scam - per well,

Can you shoe this horse o' mine? Yes, Sir,
Make the po - ny scam - per well, Scam - per,

that I can, Just as well as a - ny man.
scam - per well, Make the po - ny scam - per well.

2. There's a nail up - on the toe: The po - ny then will want to go.

There's a nail up - on the heel To make the po - ny scam - per well.

## 12. COME HOME NOW

Westphalian traditional tune, with English words by Helen Henschel

Come home now, come home now, The

bask - et's full, the work is done; Come home now, come

home now, Our work to - day is done. — We've earned our sup-per.

you'll a-gree, And we're as hung-ry as can be; Come home now, come home now, Our work to-day is done.

# 13. THE GAY MUSICIAN

German folk-song; English version by Laurence Swinyard

Verses 1.2 & 3. I am a gay mu - si - cian, I come from far a - way, I am a gay mu - si - cian, I come from far a-way. I play so gai - ly, (He plays so

(1.) Up-on my trum-pet, (Up-on his trum-pet,) Ta-
gai - ly,) (2.) Up-on my picco-lo, (Up-on his picco-lo,) (whistle-
(3.) Up-on my big drum, (Up-on his big drum,) Pom-

-ran - ta-ra, ta-ran - ta-ra, ta-ran - ta-ra - ta - ray.
- - - - - - - - - - - - - - - - - - - - - )
-pom - ti-pom, pom-pom - ti-pom, pom- pom - ti-pom-pom-pay.

*One group may sing the phrases marked A, another those marked B.

# 14. THE FOX'S SONG

# 15. ANNA MARIE

Dutch tune; words by E.L.

1. Oh, where are you go - ing, my An - na Ma - rie? Oh, where are you go - ing, my An - na Ma - rie? Go - ing to Lon - don the sol - diers to see, Go - ing to Lon - don the sol - diers to see, *Hop sa sa, fal la la, An - na Ma - rie.*

2. Oh, what are you seek - ing, my An - na Ma - rie? Oh, what are you seek - ing, my An - na Ma - rie? Seek - ing a hus - band wher - ev - er he be, Seek - ing a hus - band wher - ev - er he be, *Hop sa sa, fal la la, An - na Ma - rie.*

3. Oh, what are you look - ing for, An - na Ma - rie? Oh, what are you look - ing for, An - na Ma - rie? Look - ing for Mo - ther to get me my tea, Look - ing for Mo - ther to get me my tea, *Hop sa sa, fal la la, An - na Ma - rie.*

*Hop sa sa, fa la la, An - na Ma - rie.*

## 16. MICHAEL FINNIGIN

English traditional song

There was an old man called Mich-ael Fin-ni-gin,
was an old man called Mich-ael Fin-ni-gin,

He grew whis-kers on his chin-i-gin, The wind came up and
He kicked up an aw-ful din-i-gin, Be-cause they said he

blew them in-i-gin, Poor old Mich-ael Fin-ni-gin. (Be-gin-i-gin.) 2. There
must not sing-i-gin, Poor old Mich-ael Fin-ni-gin. (Be-gin-i-gin.) 3. There

3  There was an old man called Michael Finnigin,
   He went fishing with a pinigin,
   Caught a fish but dropped it inigin,
   Poor *etc.*

4  There was an old man called Michael Finnigin,
   Climbed a tree and barked his shinigin,
   Took off several yards of skinigin,
   Poor *etc.*

5  There was an old man called Michael Finnigin,
   He grew fat and then grew thinigin,
   Then he died, and had to beginigin,
   Poor old Michael Finnigin *STOP!* (*shouted*).

## 17. THIS OLD MAN

English traditional song

This old man he played { one,
                        { two,

He played nick-nack on my { drum.
                          { shoe.   *Nick-nack pad-dy-whack,*

14

*give a dog a bone; This old man came roll-ing home.*

3–knee  4–door  5–hive  6–sticks  7–up in heaven  8–gate  9–line  10–hen

# 18. THE KEEPER

English folk-song

Steadily    mp

1. The keep-er did a-shoot-ing go,    And
2. The first doe he shot at he missed,    The
3. The fourth doe she did cross the plain,    The

un-der his cloak he carried a bow,    All    for to shoot at a
sec-ond— doe he trimmed he kissed,    The third    doe— went where
keep-er— fetched her back a-gain,    Where she is now she—

mer-ry lit-tle doe ⎞
no - bo-dy wist ⎬  A-mong the leaves so— green    O.
may— re - main ⎠

*A      B      A      B      A      B

mf

Jack-ie Boy! Mas-ter! Sing ye well! Ve-ry well! Hey down, Ho down,

A      A+B      mp A

der-ry der-ry down,    A-mong the leaves so— green    O. To my

B      A      B

hey down down, To my ho down down,    Hey down, Ho down,

A      A+B      D.C.

mf

der-ry der-ry down,    A-mong the leaves so— green    O.

* One group may sing the phrases marked A, another those marked B.

**15**

## 19. TEN IN THE BED

English traditional song

There were | ten / nine in the bed and the lit-tle one said, "Roll o - ver! Roll o - ver!" So they all rolled o - ver and one fell out, There were

v. 2 nine, v. 3 eight etc., until the last time:
There were none in the bed, so no one said, "Roll over! Roll over!"

## 20. ONE MAN WENT TO MOW

English traditional song

One man went to mow, Went to mow a mea - dow,—
One man and his dog Went to mow a mea - dow.—
Two men went to mow, Went to mow a mea - dow,—
Three men etc.
Two men, one man, and his dog Went to mow a mea - dow.—

## 21. THERE WAS A JOLLY MILLER

English folk-song

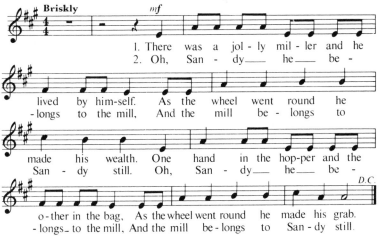

1. There was a jol-ly mil-ler and he lived by him-self. As the wheel went round he made his wealth. One hand in the hop-per and the o-ther in the bag, As the wheel went round he made his grab.

2. Oh, San-dy he be-longs to the mill, And the mill be-longs to San-dy still. Oh, San-dy he be-longs to the mill, And the mill be-longs to San-dy still.

## 22. BONEY WAS A WARRIOR

English sea shanty. 'Boney' is Napoleon Bonaparte.

1. Bo-ney was a war-ri-or, Way-ay-yah!
2. Bo-ney beat the Roo-shi-ans,

Bo-ney was a war-ri-or, John France-wah!
Bo-ney beat the Roo-shi-ans,

3  Boney beat the Prooshians,
4  Boney went to Mossycow,
5  Boney he came back again,
6  Boney went to El-be-ah,

7  Boney went to Waterloo,
8  Boney he was sent away,
9  Boney broke his heart and died,
10  Boney was a warrior.

# 23. DOWN IN DEMERARA

British student song

1. There was a man who had a hors-e-lum, had a hors-e-lum, had a hors-e-lum,
   Was a man who had a hors-e-lum, Down in De-me-ra - - ra.

2. Now that poor horse he fell a sick-e-lum, fell a sick-e-lum, fell a sick-e-lum,
   That poor horse he fell a sick-e-lum, Down in De-me-ra - - ra.

And here we sit like birds in the wil-der-ness, birds in the wil-der-ness, birds in the wil-der-ness, Here we sit like birds in the wil-der-ness, Down in De-me-ra - ra.

3  Now that poor man  he sent for a doctorum.

4  Now that poor horse  he went and diedalum.

5  And here we sit and flap our wingsalum.

**18**

# 24. DONKEY RIDING

English traditional sea song

Briskly

1. Were you e - ver in Que - bec,
2. Were you e - ver off Cape Horn,
3. Were you ever in Car - diff Bay,

Stow - ing tim - ber on the deck,   Where there's a king with a
Where it's al - ways fine and warm,   And seen the lion and the
Where the folks all shout, "Hur - ray!   Here comes John with his

gol - den crown,   Rid - ing on a don - key?
un - i - corn,   Rid - ing on a don - key?
three months' pay   Rid - ing on a don - key?"

Hey!   ho!   a - way we go,   Don - key rid - ing,

don - key   rid - ing,   Hey!____   ho!   a -

-way we go,   Rid - ing on a don - key.

**19**

# 25. WHAT SHALL WE DO WITH THE DRUNKEN SAILOR?

English sea shanty

**Not too fast**

1. What shall we do with the drunk-en sail-or,
2. Put him in the long-boat un-til he's so-ber,

What shall we do with the drunk — en sail - or,
Put him in the long - boat un - til he's so - ber,

What shall we do with the drunk — en sail - or
Put him in the long - boat un - til he's so - ber

*Ear - ly in the morn - ing? ⎱
Ear - ly in the morn - ing. ⎰ *Hoo* - *ray* *and*

*up she ris - es, Hoo - ray and up she ris - es,*

*Hoo* - *ray* *and up she ris - es* *Ear - ly in the morn - ing.*

\* pronounced 'Er-lye'

3   Pull out the plug and wet him all over.

4   Put him in the scuppers with a hose-pipe on him.

# 26. FIRE DOWN BELOW

English sea shanty

1. Fire in the gal - ley,
2. Fire in the fore - peak,

fire down be - low,⎱ It's fetch a buck - et o'
fire down be - low,⎰

wa - ter, boys, there's fire down be - low.____

Fire! fire! fire down be - low,____ It's

fetch a buck-et o' wa - ter, boys, there's fire down be - low.____

3     Fire up aloft and fire down below,
      It's fetch a bucket of water, boys, there's fire down below.
      *Fire! fire! etc.*

4     Fire in the galley, fire down below,
      It's fire in the cabin, but the captain doesn't know.
      *Fire! fire! etc.*

## 27. THE FARMYARD

English folk-song

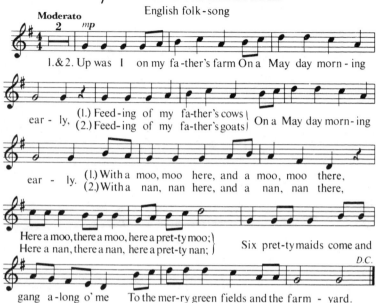

1.&2. Up was I on my fa-ther's farm On a May day morn-ing ear-ly,
(1.) Feed-ing of my fa-ther's cows ⎱
(2.) Feed-ing of my fa-ther's goats ⎰ On a May day morn-ing ear-ly.
(1.) With a moo, moo here, and a moo, moo there,
(2.) With a nan, nan here, and a nan, nan there,
Here a moo, there a moo, here a pret-ty moo; ⎱
Here a nan, there a nan, here a pret-ty nan; ⎰ Six pret-ty maids come and
gang a-long o' me To the mer-ry green fields and the farm - yard.

Other verses may be added e.g. sheep (baa baa), hens (cluck cluck).

## 28. ANDULKO

Czech folk-song ('Andulko Šafárova'), translated by Roger Fiske.
'Andulko' means 'Little angel'.

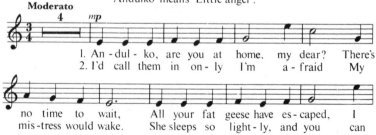

1. An - dul - ko, are you at home, my dear? There's
   no time to wait, All your fat geese have es-caped, I
2. I'd call them in on-ly I'm a - fraid My
   mis-tress would wake. She sleeps so light-ly, and you can

22

fear; They ran through the gate. All your geese
guess The trou-ble she'd make. Oh, how cross

in the corn! Call them in ere it's morn.
she can be! She would soon pu-nish me.

*mp*            *D.C.*

An-dul-ko, quick-ly come down, my dear, Be-fore it's too late.
I can't leave my lit-tle bed-room here Be-fore the day-break.

## 29. SCRAPING UP SAND

American folk-song

**Lightly**

1. Scrap-ing up sand in the bot-tom of the sea, |
2. Black those shoes and make them shine, |

Shi - loh, Shi - loh, Scrap-ing up sand in the
                                          Black those shoes and

bot-tom of the sea, | Shi - loh, Li - za Jane.
make them shine, |

Oh, how I love her, Oh, Li - za Jane,

Oh, how I love her, Good-bye, Li - za Jane.

3    Hump-backed mule I'm/bound to ride,

4    Hopped up a chicken and he/flew upstairs.

# 30. THE SHEPHERDESS

French folk-song ('*Il était une bergère*'), translated by J. Wishart

1. A shep-herd-ess was watch-ing, Ding-dong, ding-dong, ting-a-ling, ding-dong, A shep-herd-ess was watch-ing Her flock the whole day long, ding-dong, Her flock the whole day long.——

2. A cheese she made one morn-ing, Ding-dong, ding-dong, ting-a-ling, ding-dong, A cheese she made one morn-ing; Her churn turned to a song, ding-dong, Her churn turned to a song.——

3  Her pussy-cat lay winking,
   His thoughts, I fear, were wrong.

4  "If paw should touch, I'm whacking,
   With rod both stout and strong."

5  Not paw, but neck came stretching,
   To puss those lips belong.

6  The shepherdess was angry,
   Poor puss! he died ere long.

24

# 31. THE LITTLE BOY AND THE SHEEP

French folk-song ('*Je suis un petit garçon*'); English words by James Taylor

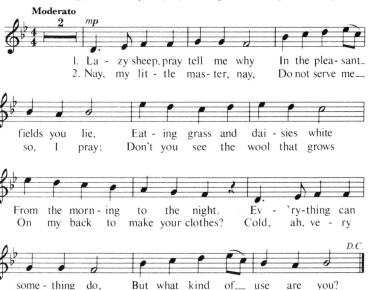

1. La - zy sheep, pray tell me why In the plea-sant fields you lie, Eat-ing grass and dai-sies white From the morn-ing to the night. Ev - 'ry-thing can some - thing do, But what kind of_ use are you?

2. Nay, my lit - tle mas-ter, nay, Do not serve me so, I pray; Don't you see the wool that grows On my back to make your clothes? Cold, ah, ve - ry cold you'd be, If you had not_ wool from me.

3   True, it seems a pleasant thing,
    Eating daisies in the Spring;
    But what chilly nights I pass
    On the cold and dewy grass,
    And sometimes the ground is bare,
    I can't find food anywhere.

4   Then the farmer comes at last,
    When the merry Spring is past;
    Cuts my woolly fleece away
    For your coat on wintry day;
    Little master, this is why
    In the pleasant fields I lie.

# 32. BOBBY SHAFTO

Northumbrian folk-song

Bob - by Shaf - to's gone to sea,— Sil - ver buck - les on his knee;— He'll come back and mar - ry me,— Bon - ny Bob - by Shaf - to.

1. Bob - by Shaf - to's bright and fair, Comb - ing down his yel - low hair; He's my ain for ev - er - mair, Bon - ny Bob - by Shaf - to.

2. Bob - by Shaf - to's tall and slim, Al - ways dress'd so neat and trim; Las - sies they all keek at him, Bon - ny Bob - by Shaf - to.

Bob - by Shaf - to's been to sea,— Sil - ver buck - les on his knee;— He's come back and mar - ried me,— Bon - ny Bob - by Shaf - to.

# 33. THE COBBLER AND THE CROW

American folk-song

Briskly     *mp*

1. There was a mer-ry cob-bler,
2. "Now, wife, you go and drive yon

bu-sy as a bee. |
dusk-y crow a-way. |

*Li - ly, li - ly, li - ly, li - ly,*

*Li - - do.*

When an old black crow came and
Or he'll perch and croak till the

perched up-on the tree. |
end-ing of the day." |

*With its Qua! Qua!*

Qua! Qua!

*Li - ly, li - ly, li - ly, li - ly, Li - do.*

D.C.

3    The cobbler's wife she tried to drive away the crow,
     But the more she tried, the more he wouldn't go.

4    Then spoke the merry cobbler at the close of day:
     "If the crow won't go, we shall have to let him stay."

# 34. THE BARNYARD SONG

American folk-song

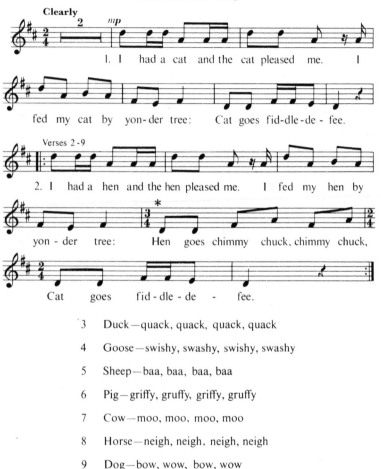

Clearly

*mp*

1. I had a cat and the cat pleased me. I fed my cat by yon-der tree: Cat goes fid-dle-de-fee.

Verses 2-9

2. I had a hen and the hen pleased me. I fed my hen by yon-der tree: Hen goes chimmy chuck, chimmy chuck, Cat goes fid-dle-de-fee.

3    Duck—quack, quack, quack, quack

4    Goose—swishy, swashy, swishy, swashy

5    Sheep—baa, baa, baa, baa

6    Pig—griffy, gruffy, griffy, gruffy

7    Cow—moo, moo, moo, moo

8    Horse—neigh, neigh, neigh, neigh

9    Dog—bow, wow, bow, wow

* Repeat this bar as required, adding the 'sounds' of a new animal in each verse.

28

# 35. TURN THE GLASSES OVER

American singing game

I've been to Har - lem, I've been to Do - ver,

I've tra - velled this wide world all o - ver,

O - ver, o - ver, three times o - ver,

Drink what you have to drink and turn the glas - ses o - ver.

Sail - ing east, sail - ing west, Sail - ing o - ver the

o - cean, Bet - ter watch out when the

boat be - gins to rock, Or you'll lose your girl in the o - cean.

# 36. GREEN GROW THE LEAVES

Northumbrian folk-song

Green grow the leaves up-on the haw-thorn tree;

Some they grow high and some they grow lee. But the

wrang-lers and the jang-lers, they nev-er can a-

-gree, And the bur-then of my song goes mer-ri-ly.

Mer-ri-ly we go, boys, mer-ri-ly we go, And the

bur-then of my song goes mer-ri-ly.

Twen-ty, nine-teen, eigh-teen, seven-teen, six-teen,

fif-teen, four-teen, thir-teen, twelve, e-lev-en,

ten, nine, eight, seven, six, five, four, three,

# 37. OH, SUSANNA

Tune and words by Stephen C. Foster

1. I came from A - la - ba - ma with my ban-jo on my knee. I'm goin' to Loui-si - a - na now, my true love for to see. It rained all night the day I left, the wea - ther it was dry; The sun so hot I froze to death; Su - san-na, don't you cry.

2. I had a dream the oth - er night, when ev - 'ry-thing was still, I thought I saw Su - san-na dear a - com - ing down the hill. The buck-wheat cake was in her mouth, a tear was in her eye; Says I, "I'm com-ing from the south; Su - san-na, don't you cry."

Oh, Su - san-na, Oh don't you cry for me; I've come from A - la - ba - ma with my ban-jo on my knee.

## 38. SHENANDOAH

American sea shanty

1. O Shen-an-doah, I long to
2. O Shen-an-doah, I love your

hear you, ) A - way, you roll-ing ri - ver! O Shen-an-
daugh-ter, )

-doah, I long to hear you;___ A -
sail - - ing 'cross the wa - ter;___ )

- way, I'm bound to go 'Cross the wide Mis - sou - ri.

3 O Shenandoah, I took a notion,
  *Away, you rolling river!*
 To sail across the briny ocean;
  *Away, I'm bound etc.*

4 O Shenandoah, I long to hear you,
  *Away, you rolling river!*
 O Shenandoah, I long to hear you;
  *Away, I'm bound etc.*

## 39. THE ANIMALS WENT IN TWO BY TWO

English traditional song

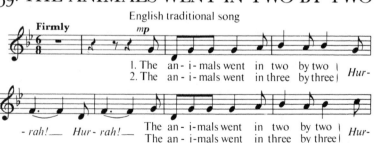

1. The an - i - mals went in two by two )
2. The an - i - mals went in three by three ) Hur-

- rah!___ Hur - rah!___ The an - i - mals went in two by two ) Hur-
The an - i - mals went in three by three )

**32**

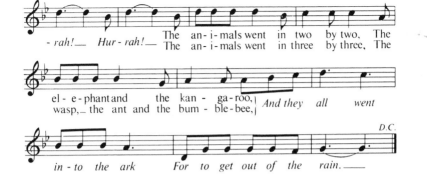

-rah!___ Hur-rah!___ The an-i-mals went in two by two, The
The an-i-mals went in three by three, The

el-e-phant and the kan-ga-roo, | And they all went
wasp,_ the ant and the bum-ble-bee, | 

in-to the ark For to get out of the rain.___ *D.C.*

3    The animals went in four by four
        *Hurrah! hurrah!*
    The animals went in four by four
        *Hurrah! hurrah!*
    The animals went in four by four:
    The great hippopotamus stuck in the door,
        *And they all etc.*

4    The animals went in five by five
        *Hurrah! hurrah!*
    The animals went in five by five
        *Hurrah! hurrah!*
    The animals went in five by five:
    By eating each other they kept alive,
        *And they all etc.*

5    The animals went in six by six
        *Hurrah! hurrah!*
    The animals went in six by six
        *Hurrah! hurrah!*
    The animals went in six by six:
    They turned out the monkey because of his tricks,
        *And they all etc.*

6    The animals went in seven by seven
        *Hurrah! hurrah!*
    The animals went in seven by seven
        *Hurrah! hurrah!*
    The animals went in seven by seven:
    The little pig thought he was going to heaven,
        *And they all etc.*

# 40. LI'L LIZA JANE

American traditional song

Lightly

1. I know a gal that you don't know,
2. Li - za___ Jane looks good to me,

Li'l Li - za Jane,

'Way down south in
Sweet - est one I

Bal - ti - mo,'
ev - er see,

Li'l Li - za Jane,

Oh, E - li - za, li'l Li - za Jane,

Oh, E - li - za, li'l Li - za Jane!

D.C.

3  Where she lives the posies grow,
   Chickens roun' the kitchen do'.

4  What do I care how far we roam?
   Where she's at is home, sweet home.

34

# 41. SACRAMENTO

Sea shanty

1. A - round Cape Horn we're bound to go,
2. A - round Cape Horn in the month of May,
3. To the Sac - ra - men - to we're bound a - way,

*Sac-ra-men-to, Sac-ra-men-to,*

A -
A -
To the

- round Cape Horn thro' sleet and snow
- round Cape Horn is a very long way
Sac - ra - men - to's a long, long way.

*To the*

banks o' Sac - ra-men-to. Blow, boys,_ blow, for

Cal - i - for - nia, O! There's plen-ty o' gold so

I've been told On the banks o' Sac - ra-men - to.

35

# 42. SALLY BROWN

American sea shanty.
'Mulatter' is 'mulatto', of mixed white and negro blood.

1. Sal - ly Brown she's a bright mu - lat - ter,
2. Sev'n long years I court - ed Sal - ly,

Way - ay - y roll and go;

She drinks rum and
Sev'n long years I

*Verses 1 to 4*

chews ter - bac-cer,
court - ed Sal - ly,

Spend my mo-ney on Sal - ly Brown.

*Last verse*

Spend my mo - ney on Sal - ly Brown.

3  Sally Brown she has a daughter,
       *Way-ay-y roll and go;*
   Sent me sailing 'cross the water,
       Spend my money on Sally Brown.

4  Sally lives on the old plantation,
       *Way-ay-y roll and go;*
   She's a girl of the Wild Goose nation,
       Spend my money on Sally Brown.

5  Sally Brown she's a bright mulatter,
       *Way-ay-y roll and go;*
   She drinks rum and chews terbaccer,
       Spend my money on Sally Brown.

# 43. THE SMUGGLER'S SONG

Old English tune, with words by Huw Lewis

# 44. RIO GRANDE

British sea shanty.
The Rio Grande is a river in Brazil, not the North American river.

**Moderato**

1. Oh, where are you go - ing,
   may I go with you,

my pret - ty maid? )
my pret - ty maid? )   *Oh,_____ Ri - o!_____* "I'm
                                                      "You're

go - ing a - milk - ing, Sir,"_ she said, )
kind - ly wel - come, Sir,"_ she said, )   *But we're*

*bound for the Ri - o Grande. Then a -*

*-way, love,_ a - way,_____ 'Way,_____ for*

*Ri - o,_____ So fare___ you well,___ my*

bon - ny young girl, For we're bound for the Ri - o

*All verses except the last*        *D.S.* ‖ *Last time*

*Grande.*                 2. Oh,    *Grande.___*

3    Oh, what is your father, my pretty maid?
        *Oh, Rio,*
     "My father's a farmer, Sir," she said,
        *But we're bound etc.*

4    Oh, pray will you marry me, my pretty maid?
        *Oh, Rio,*
     "I will if you wish, kind Sir," she said,
        *But we're bound etc.*

5    Oh, what is your fortune, my pretty maid?
        *Oh, Rio,*
     "My face is my fortune, Sir," she said,
        *But we're bound etc.*

6    Oh, then I can't marry you, my pretty maid,
        *Oh, Rio,*
     "Oh, nobody asked you, Sir," she said,
        *But we're bound etc.*

# 45. SWEET NIGHTINGALE

English folk-song

1. My sweet-heart, come a - long, Don't you
2. Pret-ty Bet - ty, don't fail, For I'll

hear the fond song, The sweet notes of the night-in-gale flow?__
car - ry your pail Safe__ home to your cot as we go.__

__ Don't you \
__ You shall / hear the fond tale of the sweet night-in-gale, As she

sings in the val - ley be - low, _____

__ As she sings in the val - ley be - low(?)_____

3 "Pray let me alone,
  I have hands of my own,
  Along with you, Sir, I'll not go
    *For to hear the fond tale*" *etc.*

4 Pray sit yourself down
  With me on the ground,
  On this bank where the primroses grow,
    *You shall hear the fond tale etc.*

5 The couple agreed
  To be married with speed,
  And soon to the church they did go.
  No more is she afraid
  For to walk in the shade
    *Or to sit in those valleys below,*
    *Or to sit in those valleys below.*

**40**

# 46. LEAVE HER, JOHNNY

British sea shanty

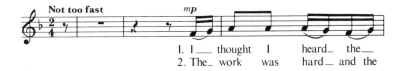

**Not too fast**   *mp*

1. I ___ thought   I      heard ___ the ___
2. The ___ work   was    hard ___ and the

skip  -  per ___  say, ⎫
pas  -  sage ___ long, ⎬   *Leave   her,   John  -  ny,*

*leave      her!*   "To  -  mor  -  row   you   will
The   seas   were   high   and the

D.C.

get   your ___ pay:" ⎫
gales  were strong, ⎬  *It's   time   for   us      to   leave   her.*

3   The food was bad and the wages low,
    But now ashore again we'll go.

4   The sails are furled and our work is done,
    And now on shore we'll have some fun.

# 47. PRETTY POLLY OLIVER

17th-century English song

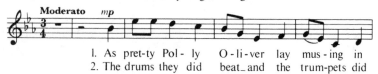

1. As pret-ty Pol - ly O - li-ver lay mus-ing in
2. The drums they did beat and the trum-pets did

bed, A com - i - cal fan - cy came in - to her
blow When Pol - ly in un-i-form to the war she did

head: "Nor fa - ther nor moth - er shall make me false
go, Her lo - ver was wound-ed and fell by her

prove, I'll 'list for a sol - dier and fol - low my love."
side, And, as Pol-ly lift-ed him, she knew that he had died.

3  Poor Polly sat crying, dead soldiers all around,

When up came the Captain, who said as he frowned:

"A soldier here weeping, a soldier afraid?"

"Oh, Sir! I'm no soldier," said Polly, "I'm a maid."

4  "A maid?" said the Captain, "then throw her in jail."

"Oh, no," pleaded Polly, who told her sad tale,

And when a great vic-t'ry had ended the strife

The Captain took Polly and made her his wife.

# 48. ROBIN ADAIR

Irish tune, with words attributed to Robert Burns

**Fairly slowly**

1. What's this dull town to me? Ro - bin's not
2. What made th'as - semb - ly shine? Ro - bin A -
3. But now thou`rt cold to me, Ro - bin A -

near. What was't I wished to see, What wished to
-dair. What made the ball so fine? Ro - bin was
-dair. But now thou`rt cold to me, Ro - bin A -

hear? Where all the joy and mirth
there. What when the play was o'er,
-dair. Yet he I loved so well

Made this town heav'n on earth? Oh, they're_all_
What made my heart so sore? Oh, it _ was_
Still in my heart shall dwell; Oh, I _ can_

fled with thee, Ro - bin A - dair.
part - ing with Ro - bin A - dair.
ne'er for - get Ro - bin A - dair.

43

## 49. O RARE TURPIN

English traditional song. The narrator is Turpin.

Moderato    mf

1. On Houn - slow Heath as
2. Says Tur - pin, "He'll ne'er

I rode— o'er, I spied a law - yer
find me— out. I've hid my mon - ey

ri - ding be - fore. "Kind— Sir," said I, "aren't
in my— boot." The— law - yer says, "There's

you a - fraid Of Tur - pin, that mis - chiev - ous—blade?"
none can find My gold stitched in my— cape— be - hind."

O rare Tur - pin he - ro, O rare Tur - pin,— O.

3    As they rode by the powder mill
Our Turpin bids him to stand still,
Says he, "Your cape I must cut off,
My mare she wants a saddle cloth."

4    This caused the lawyer much to fret
To think he was so fairly hit;
And Turpin robbed him of his store,
Because he knew he'd lie for more.

44

# 50. THE LASS OF RICHMOND HILL

Tune by J. Hook, words by W. Upton.
The poem honours a 'lass' who lived in Richmond, Yorkshire.

1. On Rich-mond Hill there lives_a__ lass, More
2. How hap - py will the lo - ver__ be Who

bright than May - day morn,_____ Whose charms all oth - er
calls the maid his own, _____ O may her choice be

maids_ sur - pass, A rose with - out a thorn.|
fixed__ on__ me, Mine's fixed on her a - lone. |    This

lass so neat, with smiles so sweet, Has won my right good will, __ I'd

crowns re - sign to call thee mine, Sweet lass of Rich-mond Hill;    Sweet

lass of Rich-mond Hill, Sweet lass of Rich-mond Hill, I'd

crowns re-sign to call thee mine, Sweet lass of Rich-mond Hill.

# 51. THE LINCOLNSHIRE POACHER

English traditional song

1. When I was bound ap-
2. As me and my com-

-pren - tice, in fam - ous Lin - coln - shire,____ Full
-pan - i - ons were set - ting of a snare,____ 'Twas

well I served my mas - ter for more than sev - en
then we spied the game - keep-er, for him we did__ not

year,____ Till I took up to poach - ing, as
care,____ For we can wrestle and fight, my boys, and

you shall quick - ly hear; }
jump o'er an - y - where; }   *Oh! 'tis my de - light on a*

**46**

shin - ing night in the sea - son of the year. Oh!___

'tis my de - light on a

shin - ing night in the sea - son of the year.___

3    As me and my companions were setting four or five,
    And taking on 'em up again, we caught a hare alive,
    We took the hare alive, my boys, and through the woods did steer;
        *Oh, 'tis my delight etc.*

4    I took him on my shoulder, and then we trudgèd home,
    We took him to a neighbour's house and sold him for a crown,
    We sold him for a crown, my boys, I did not tell you where;
        *Oh, 'tis my delight etc.*

5    Success to every gentleman who lives in Lincolnshire,
    Success to every poacher who wants to sell a hare,
    Bad luck to every gamekeeper who will not sell his deer;
        *Oh, 'tis my delight etc.*

## 52. I'SE THE B'Y THAT BUILDS THE BOAT

Newfoundland folk-song

Moderato

1. I'se the b'y that builds the boat, I'se the b'y that
2. Flour and crumbs to cover your fish, Cake and tea for

sails her! I'se the b'y that catch-es the fish And
sup - per, Cod fish in the spring o' the year___

takes them home to Li - za.) *Hip yer part - ner, Sal - ly Tib-bo,*
Fried in ran - cid but - ter. )

*Hip yer part - ner, Sal - ly Brown!* *Fo - go, Twill - in - gate,

*More - ton's Har - bour, All a - round the cir - cle!*

D.C.

3  I don't want your rancid fish,
    That's no good for winter;
  I could buy as good as that
    Down in Bonavista.
    *Hip yer partner, etc.*

4  I took Liza to a dance,
    And faith, but she could travel!
  Every step that she did take
    Was up to her knees in gravel.
    *Hip yer partner, etc.*

5  Susan White, she's out of sight,
    Her petticoat wants a border;
  Old Sam Oliver in the dark
    He kissed her in the corner.
    *Hip yer partner, etc.*

*The places mentioned are ports round Notre Dame Bay in N.E.
Newfoundland.

# 53. JOHN BARLEYCORN

Somerset folk-song

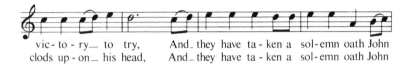

1. There came three men from_ out the west Their
2. They took a plough 'and_ploughed him in, Laid

vic-to-ry_ to try, And_ they have ta-ken a sol-emn oath John
clods up-on_ his head, And_ they have ta-ken a sol-emn oath John

Bar - ley-corn should die._ ⎱ Sing ri - fol - lol, the
Bar - ley-corn is dead._ ⎰

did-dle all the dee, Right fal-lee - ro - dee.

3  So then he lay for three long weeks
      Till dew from heaven did fall;
   John Barleycorn sprang up again
      And that surprised them all.

4  There he remained till midsummer
      And looked both pale and wan,
   For all he had a spikey beard
      To show he was a man.

5  But soon men came with their sharp scythes
      And chopped him to the knee;
   They rolled and tied him by the waist
      And served him barbarously.

49

# 54. HOPE, THE HERMIT

English 17th-century tune; words by John Oxenford

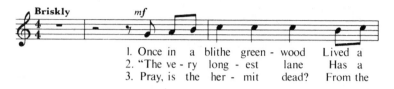

Briskly     *mf*

1. Once in a blithe green-wood Lived a
2. "The ve-ry long-est lane Has a
3. Pray, is the her-mit dead? From the

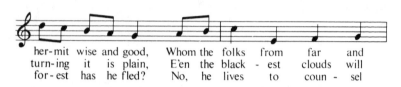

her-mit wise and good, Whom the folks from far and
turn-ing it is plain, E'en the black-est clouds will
for-est has he fled? No, he lives to coun-sel

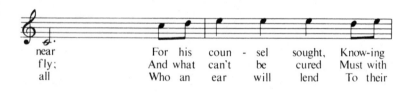

near     For his coun-sel sought, Know-ing
fly;     And what can't be cured Must with
all     Who an ear will lend To their

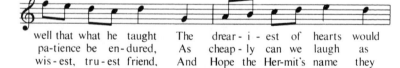

well that what he taught The drear-i-est of hearts would
pa-tience be en-dured, As cheap-ly can we laugh as
wis-est, tru-est friend, And Hope the Her-mit's name they

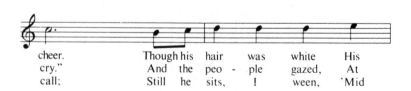

cheer.     Though his hair was white His
cry."     And the peo-ple gazed, At
call;     Still he sits, I ween, 'Mid

eye was clear and bright, And he thus was ev- er wont to
words so deep, am- azed, While the sage__ went__ on to
bran-ches ev - er green, And__ cheer- ly you may hear him

say: ⎫
say: ⎬ "Though to care we are born, Yet the
say: ⎭

dull - est morn Oft- en her- alds in the fair - est

*f*

day, Though to care we are born, Yet the

*D.C.*

dull - est morn Oft- en her-alds in the fair - est day!"

# 55. HO-LA-HI

German folk-song, translated by Elizabeth Fiske

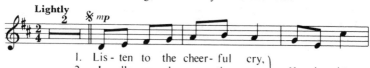

Lightly

1. Lis - ten to the cheer- ful cry,
2. I - dle peo - ple ques - tion me,  } Ho - la - hi,
3. Spite-ful peo - ple some-times hiss,

ho - la - ho,  Is my sweet - heart pass-ing by? }
What my true love's name can be,  } Ho- la - hi - a -
No-thing good can come of this,

- ho!  No, the voice fades down the street,
Let them won - der, let them tease,  }
She will ne - ver be your own,

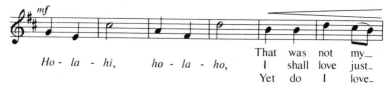

Ho - la - hi,  ho - la - ho,  That was not my
I shall love just
Yet do I love

dar - ling sweet,
as I please,  } Ho - la - hi - a - ho!
her a - lone,

52

# 56. FISHERMAN'S NIGHT SONG

Irish folk-song, with words by L. A. G. Strong

1. In the calm— hour of
2. Let us sit —— by the

eve— ning When the sea— gulls fly slow To their
fire - side And re - mem - ber our friends. Each——

rocks on the— is - land And— cry as they
day ends in —— dark - ness But— hope ne - ver

go, From each house on the— head - land Lights be -
ends. When the last shoal is —— ta - ken And the

- gin to twin-kle in the gloom, And the pale— cold world
last— boat— comes to shore, We will all —— sing to -

dwin - dles To a warm— qui - et room.
-geth - er, Di - vi - ded no more.

# 57. FAREWELL, MANCHESTER!

Tune by Rev. William Felton (1713-1769), and said to have been played when the Young Pretender's army left Manchester in 1747. Words by John Oxenford.

**Not too slowly**

1. Fare - well, Man - ches - ter! no - ble town, fare-
2. Fare - well, Man - ches - ter! sad - ly I de-

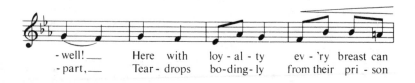

- well!___ Here with loy - al - ty ev - 'ry breast can
- part,___ Tear - drops bo - ding - ly from their pri - son

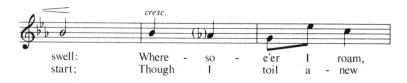

swell: Where - so - e'er I roam,
start; Though I toil a - new

Here, as in a home, Ev - er, dear
Sha - dows to pur - sue, Sha - dows vain—

Lan - ca - shire, My heart_____ shall dwell.
thou'lt re - main With - in_____ my heart.

54

# 58. FAITHFUL JOHNNY

Scottish traditional song

1. When will you come a - gain?
2. Then win - ter's wind will blow,
3. Then will you meet me here?

When will you
Then win - ter's
Then will you

come a - gain?
wind will blow,
meet me here?

My___ faith - ful John - ny;

When the_ corn is ga - ther - ed, When the_ leaves are
Though the_ day be dark with_ drift, That I__ can - not
Though the_ night were Hal - low - een, When the_ fear - ful

wi - ther - ed,
see the_ lift,
sights are_ seen,

I will come a - gain,

My___ sweet and bon - ny, I will come a - gain.__

55

# 59. ELSIE MARLEY

Tune by Thomas Dunhill, with traditional English words

Do you ken El - sie Mar - ley, hon-ey, The wife that sells the bar - ley, hon-ey, The wife that sells the bar - ley? Do you ken El - sie, Do you ken El - sie, Do you ken El - sie Mar - ley? El - sie Mar - ley's grown so fine_ She won't get up to feed the swine, But lies in bed till eight or nine, And sure - ly she_ does take her time._____ Do you ken El - sie Mar - ley, hon-ey, The wife that sells the bar - ley, hon-ey, The wife, the wife, the wife that sells the bar - ley?

# 60. EARLY ONE MORNING

English folk-song

**Moderato**

1. Ear - ly one morn - ing just
2. "Gay is the gar - land and
3. Thus sang the maid - en, her

as the sun was ri - sing, I heard a maid - en
fresh__ are the ro - ses I've culled__ from the
sor - rows be - wail - ing, Thus sang the poor__

sing__ in the val - ley be - low:
gar - den to bind__ on your brow:"
maid__ in the val - ley be - low:

"Oh, don't de - ceive__ me, Oh, ne - ver leave__ me,

*D.C.*

How__ could you use__ a __ poor__ maid - en so?"

# 61. CAPTAIN MORGAN'S MARCH

Welsh folk-song, 'Rhyfelgyrch Capten Morgan'.
English version by J. B. P. Dobbs.

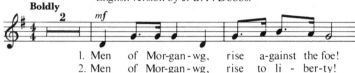

1. Men of Mor-gan-wg, rise a-gainst the foe!
2. Men of Mor-gan-wg, rise to li - ber-ty!

Send him hence or lay him low,
Cym - ru now shall soon be free,

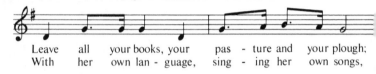

Leave all your books, your pas - ture and your plough;
With her own lan - guage, sing - ing her own songs,

Gird on wea - pons, join us now. )
Right - ing all her conq - 'ror's wrongs. |

Mor - gan calls you, bids you with him stand,

Drive the raid - ing Sa - xon from this fair land.

Pronunciation: *Morganwg* = Morganoog  *Cymru* = Kumri

58

# 62. THE CUCKOO

Austrian folk-song, with words by Katherine F. Rohrbaugh

1. Oh, I went to Pe-ter's
2. Af-ter East-er come—
3. When I've mar-ried my—

flow-ing spring Where the wa-ter's so good; And I
sun-ny days That will melt all the snow; Then I'll
maid-en fair What then can I de-sire? Oh, a

heard there the cuck-oo As he called from the wood.
mar-ry my maid-en fair: We'll be hap-py, I know.
home for her ten-ding And some wood for the fire.

Ho - li - ah,   Ho - le-rah-hi-hi-ah, Ho-le-rah ku-kuck,

Ho - le-rah-hi - hi-ah, Ho - le-rah ku-kuck, Ho - le-rah-hi-hi-ah,

Ho - le-rah ku-kuck,   Ho - le-rah - hi-hi-ah ho.

# 63. THE BRITISH GRENADIERS

English traditional song

1. Some talk of Al - ex - an - der, And some of Her - cu - les, Of Hec - tor and Ly - san - der, And such great names as these; But of all the world's brave he - roes There's none that can com - pare. With a tow, row, row, row, row, row, For the Brit - ish Gre - na - diers.

2. And when the siege is ov - er, We to the town re - pair. The towns - men cry, "Hur - rah, boys, Here come the Gre - na - diers; Here come the Gre - na - diers, my boys, Who know no doubts or fears," With a tow, row, row, row, row, row, For the Brit - ish Gre - na - diers.

3. Then let us fill a bum - per, And drink a health to those Who car - ry caps and pou - ches, And wear the lou - ped clothes; May they and their com - man - ders Live hap - py all their years, With a tow, row, row, row, row, row, For the Brit - ish Gre - na - diers.

# 64. COCKLES AND MUSSELS

Irish traditional song

# 65. BARBARA ALLEN

English traditional song

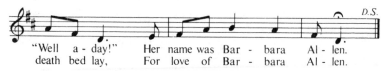

1. In Scar-let Town, where I was born, There was a fair maid dwell-ing,__ Made ev'-ry youth cry,__ "Well a - day!" Her name was Bar - bara Al - len.

2. All in the mer - ry month of May, When green buds they were swell-ing,__ Young Jem-my Grove on his death bed lay, For love of Bar - bara Al - len.

3     So slowly, slowly she came up,
        And slowly she came nigh him;
    And all she said, when there she came:
        "Young man, I think you're dying."

4     When he was dead and laid in grave,
        Her heart was struck with sorrow;
    "O mother, mother, make my bed,
        For I shall die tomorrow!"

5     "Farewell," she said, "ye maidens all,
        And shun the fault I fell in;
    Henceforth take warning by the fall
        Of cruel Barbara Allen."

# 66. CHARLIE IS MY DARLING

Scottish traditional tune, with words by Lady Nairne

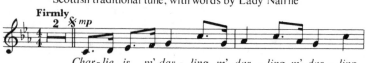

*Char-lie is m' dar - ling, m' dar - ling, m' dar - ling,*

*Char-lie is m' dar - ling, the young Chev-a-lier.*

mf

1. 'Twas
2. As

on   a Mon-day morn - ing Right ear - ly  in   the year,   When
he came march-ing up the street, The pipes played loud and clear,   And

D.S. for vv. 2, 3, 4.

Char-lie came to   our__ town, The_ young_Chev - a-lier,⎫  Oh!
all   the folks came run-ning out   To_ meet the Chev - a-lier,⎭

After v. 4

mp

*Char - lie  is   m' dar - ling, m' dar - ling, m' dar - ling,*

*Char - lie  is   m' dar - ling, the young   Chev - a - lier.*

3   Wi' Hieland bonnets on their heads,
        And claymores bright and clear,
    They came to fight for Scotland's right,
        And for the Chevalier.
            *Oh! Charlie etc.*

4   They've left their bonnie Hieland hills,
        Their wives and *children dear,
    To draw the sword for Scotland's Lord,
        The young Chevalier.
            *Oh! Charlie etc.*

*or 'bairnies'

**63**

# 67. CADER IDRIS

Welsh folk-song, with words by Jacqueline Froom.
'Cader Idris' is the name of a mountain.

1. Light-heart-ed I stroll through the Vale of Llan-goll-en, And climb the steep moun - tain, ad - mir - ing the view. All round me the moun - tains roll on - ward and on - ward, Till dis - tance has changed all their green in - to blue. I__ see the clear streams tum - bling down the__ steep__ hill - side, And wa - ter - falls spill - ing their mist from a height; I__ see a white cot - tage be - low by the birch-grove, And mem-'ries of child - hood come shin - ing and bright.

2. Light - foot - ed I leap down the side of the moun - tain, My heart beat - ing fas - ter with thoughts of the past: How hap - py my life in that cot - tage be - low me, How hap - py the years that raced on - ward so fast! I__ lived in that cot - tage with fa - ther__ and__ mo - ther, And sis - ters and bro - thers were gath - ered a - round. But__ now all for - sa - ken, for - lorn and de - ser - ted, The cot - tage is crum - bling, and this - tles a - bound.

64

# 68. BLOW AWAY THE MORNING DEW

Somerset folk-song

1. Up - on the sweet-est sum-mer-time In the
2. She gath-ered to her love - ly flowers And

mid - dle of the morn, A pret-ty dam-sel I es - pied, The
spent her time in sport, As if in pret - ty Cu- pid's bowers She

fair - est ev - er born.⎱
dai - ly did re - sort.⎰   *And sing blow     a - way the*

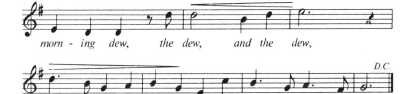

*morn - ing dew,     the dew,     and the   dew,*

*Blow     a - way the morn - ing dew, How sweet     the winds  do  blow.*

```
3    The yellow cowslip by the brim,
         The daffodil as well,
     The timid primrose, pale and trim,
         The pretty snowdrop bell.
             And sing etc.

4    She's gone with all those flowers sweet
         Of white and red and blue,
     And unto me about my feet
         Is only left the rue.
             And sing etc.
```

# 69. AFTON WATER

Scottish traditional tune, with words by Robert Burns

1. Flow gen - tly, sweet Af - ton, a -
2. Thou stock - dove, whose ech - o re -

-mong thy green braes, Flow gen - tly, I'll sing thee a -
-sounds through the glen, Ye wild, whist - ling black-birds in

song in thy praise; My Ma - ry's a -
yon thorn - y den, Thou green - crest - ed

- sleep by thy mur - mur - ing stream, Flow
lap - wing, thy scream - ing for - bear, I

gen - tly, sweet Af - ton, di - sturb not her dream.
charge you di - sturb not my slum - ber - ing fair.

# 70. THE ASH GROVE

Welsh traditional tune, with words by Thomas Oliphant

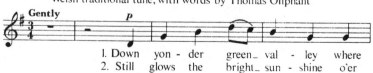

1. Down yon - der green - val - ley where
2. Still glows the bright sun - shine o'er

stream - lets\_ me - an - der, When twi - light\_ is\_
val - ley\_ and\_ moun - tain, Still war - bles\_ the\_

fa - ding, I pen - sive - ly rove; Or at the bright\_
black - bird its notes from the tree; Still trem - bles the\_\_

noon - tide, in sol - i - tude\_wan - der A - mid the\_ dark\_
moon - beam on stream - let\_ and\_foun - tain, But what are\_ the\_\_

*mp*
shades of the lone - ly Ash Grove. 'Twas\_there, while\_the\_
beau - ties of na - ture to me? With\_ sor - row,\_deep\_

black - bird was cheer - ful - ly\_ sing - ing, I
sor - row, my bo - som\_ is\_ la - den, All

*p*
first met\_ that\_ dear one, the joy of my heart! A -
day I\_\_ go\_\_mourn - ing in search of my love; Ye

-round us for\_ glad - ness the blue - bells\_ were\_ring - ing; Ah!
ech - oes! oh\_ tell me, where is the\_ sweet\_mai - den? "She

*D.C.*
then lit - tle\_thought I how soon we should part.
sleeps 'neath\_the\_ green turf down by the Ash Grove."

# 71. A-ROVING

English sea shanty

**Moderato**

1. In Am - ster - dam there
2. Her cheeks were red, her
3. I put my arm a -

lived a maid,
eyes were brown, } *Mark well what I do say;*
-round her waist,

In
Her
I

Am - ster - dam there lived a maid, And she was mis - tress
cheeks were red, her eyes were brown, Her hair so black was
put my arm a - round her waist, Says she, "Young man, you're

of her trade, }
hang - ing down, } *I'll go no more a - rov - ing with*
in great haste!"

you, fair maid. A - rov - ing, a -

- rov - ing, Since rov - ing's been my ru - i - in, I'll

**68**

go no more a - rov - ing with you, fair maid.

## 72. GOLDEN SLUMBERS

English 17th-century song

1. Gold - en slum - bers kiss your
2. Care you know not, there - fore

eyes, Smiles a - wake you
sleep, While I o'er you

when you rise; Sleep, pret - ty maid - en,
watch do keep; Sleep, pret - ty darl - ing,

do not cry, And I will
do not cry, And I will

sing a lul - la - - by.
sing a lul - la - - by.

**69**

# 73. THE TREE IN THE WOOD

Somerset folk-song

1. All in a wood there grew a tree, The fin - est tree you ev - er did see, And the green leaves grew a - round, a-round, a-round, And the green leaves grew a - round.   2. And on this tree there was a limb, The fin - est limb you ev-er did see, The limb was on the tree, The tree was in the wood, And the green leaves grew a- round, a-round, a-round, And the green leaves grew a - round.   3. And -round.

Verses 3 to 9

Verses 2 to 8   D.S. Last time

\* This bar is sung twice in the 3rd verse, three times in the 4th verse etc.

70

3    And ON this limb there was a branch,
     The finest branch you ever did see,
                    (*to 3 below*)

4    And ON this branch there was a nest,
     The finest nest *etc.*      (*to 4*)

5    And IN  this nest there was an egg,
     The finest egg *etc.*       (*to 5*)

6    And IN this egg there was a yolk,
     The finest yolk *etc.*      (*to 6*)

7    And IN this yolk there was a bird,
     The finest bird *etc.*      (*to 7*)

8    And ON this bird there was a wing,
     The finest wing *etc.*      (*to 8*)

9    And ON this wing there was a feather,
     The finest feather *etc.*   (*to 9*)


9    The feather was ON the wing,
8    The wing was ON the bird,
7    The bird was IN the yolk,
6    The yolk was IN the egg,
5    The egg was IN the nest,
*4*    The nest was ON the branch,
*3*    The branch was ON the limb,
*2*    The limb was ON the tree,
*1*    The tree was IN the wood,
     *And the green leaves etc.*

# 74. GREEN GROW THE RUSHES, HO!

English traditional song

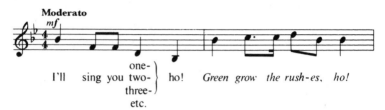

I'll sing you one-
two-
three-
etc.
} ho! *Green grow the rush-es, ho!*

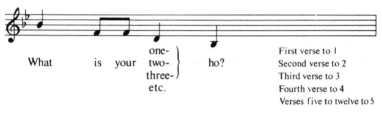

What is your one-
two-
three-
etc.
} ho?

First verse to 1
Second verse to 2
Third verse to 3
Fourth verse to 4
Verses five to twelve to 5

**1**
One is one and all a - lone and ev - er more shall be so.

**2**
Two, two the li - ly-white boys, cloth-ed all in green_ ho,

One is one and all a - lone and ev - er more shall be so.

72

Three,      three    the    ri  -  vals,

Four    for    the    Gos - pel    mak -  -  ers,

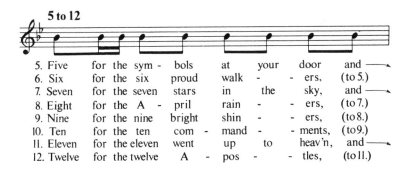

5. Five    for the sym -  bols    at    your    door    and
6. Six      for the six    proud    walk -  -  ers,    (to 5.)
7. Seven  for the seven  stars    in    the    sky,    and
8. Eight   for the A -  pril    rain -  -  ers,    (to 7.)
9. Nine    for the nine  bright    shin -  -  ers,    (to 8.)
10. Ten    for the ten   com -  mand -  -  ments,    (to 9.)
11. Eleven  for the eleven  went    up    to    heav'n,    and
12. Twelve  for the twelve  A -  pos -  -  tles,    (to 11.)

Four    for    the    Gos - pel    mak -  -  ers,

Six    for    the    six    proud    walk -  -  ers,  (to 5.)

Ten    for    the    ten    com -  mand -  -  ments, (to 9.)

# 75. MARCHING THROUGH GEORGIA

Tune and words by Henry C. Work (American Civil War song)

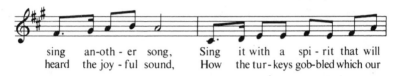

1. Bring the good old bu - gle, boys, we'll
2. How the dark - ies shout - ed when they

sing an-oth - er song, Sing it with a spi - rit that will
heard the joy - ful sound, How the tur - keys gob-bled which our

start the world a - long, Sing it as we used to sing it
Comm - iss - a - ry found; How the sweet po - ta - toes ev - en

fif - ty thou - sand strong,⎫
start - ed from the ground,⎭ While we were march - ing through

Geor - gia. Hur - rah! hur - rah! we bring the Jub - i - lee! Hur-

-rah! hur - rah! the flag that makes you free!

*So we sang the cho-rus from At-lan-ta to the sea,*

*While we were march-ing through Geor - gia!*

D.C.

3    Yes, and there were Union men who wept with joyful tears,
     When they saw the honoured flag they had not seen for years;
     Hardly could they be restrained from breaking into cheers,
          *While we were etc.*

4    "Sherman's dashing Yankee boys will never reach the coast,"
     So the saucy rebels said, and 'twas a handsome boast;
     Had they not forgot, alas, to reckon with the host,
          *While we were etc.*

5    So we made a thoroughfare for freedom and her train,
     Sixty miles in latitude, three hundred to the main;
     Treason fled before us, for resistance was in vain,
          *While we were etc.*

# 76. JOHN BROWN'S BODY

March song of the American Civil War

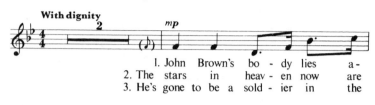

1. John Brown's bo - dy lies a -
2. The stars in heav - en now are
3. He's gone to be a sold - ier in the

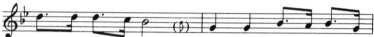

- mould -'ring in the grave, John Brown's bo - dy lies a -
look - ing kind - ly down, The stars in heav - en now are
ar - my of the Lord, He's gone to be a sold - ier in the

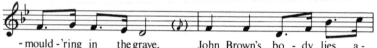

- mould -'ring in the grave, John Brown's bo - dy lies a -
look - ing kind - ly down, The stars in heav - en now are
ar - my of the Lord, He's gone to be a sold - ier in the

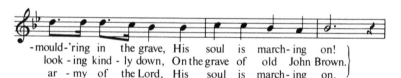

- mould-'ring in the grave, His soul is march-ing on!
look - ing kind - ly down, On the grave of old John Brown.
ar - my of the Lord, His soul is march-ing on.

Glo - ry, Glo - ry, Hal-le - lu - jah! Glo - ry, Glo - ry, Hal - le - lu - jah!

Glo - ry, Glo - ry, Hal - le - lu - jah! His soul is march-ing on!

## 77. JENNIE JENKINS

American singing game

**Merrily**

1. O will you wear white, O my dear, O my dear? O will you wear white, Jen-nie Jen-kins? I won't wear white, for the col-our's too bright,
2. O will you wear red, O my dear, O my dear? O will you wear red, Jen-nie Jen-kins? I won't wear red, it's the col-our of my head,

*I'll buy me a fol-di-rol-dy, til-di-tol-dy, seek a dou-ble, use a cause-a-roll to bind me.* Roll, roll, roll, Jen-nie Jen-kins roll.— roll.— roll!

3  O will you wear green?
   I won't wear green, it's a shame to be seen.

4  O will you wear blue?
   I won't wear blue, I'd be just like you.

77

# 78. CAMPTOWN RACES

Tune and words by Stephen C. Foster

**Briskly**

1. The Camp-town la - dies sing this song,
2. The long - tail filly and the big black hoss,

*Doo - dah!_ doo - dah!_* The Camp-town race-track five miles long,
*Doo - dah!_ doo - dah!_* They fly the track an' they both cut a-cross,

*Oh! doo-dah day!* I come down there wid my hat caved in,
*Oh! doo-dah day!* The blind hoss sticking in a big mud hole,

*Doo - dah!_ doo - dah!_* I go back home wid a pocket full of tin,
*Doo - dah!_ doo - dah!_* Can't touch the bottom wid a ten - foot pole,

*Oh! doo - dah day!*
*Oh! doo - dah day!* } *Gwine to run all night!*

*Gwine to run all day!* I'll_ bet my mo-ney on the

bob - tail nag, Some - bo-dy bet on the bay.

3  Old muley cow come on the track,
   The bobtail fling her over his back,
   Then fly along like a railroad car,
   And run a race wid a shootin' star,
   *Oh! Doodah day!*
   *Gwine to run etc.*

4    Oh, see them flyin' on a ten-mile heat
      Around the race-track then repeat,
      I win my money on the bob-tail nag,
      I keep my money in an old tow bag,
      *Oh! Doodah day!*
      *Gwine to run etc.*

# 79. YE BANKS AND BRAES

Scottish traditional tune, with words by Robert Burns

1. Ye banks and braes o' bonnie Doon, How can ye bloom sae fresh and fair? How can ye chant, ye little birds, And I sae weary, fu' o' care? Thou'lt break my heart, thou warbling bird, That wantons through the flow'ring thorn, Thou minds me o' departed joys, Departed never to return.

2. Oft hae I roved by bonnie Doon, To see the rose and woodbine twine, And ilka bird sang o' its love, And fondly sae did I o' mine. Wi' lightsome heart I pu'd a rose, Fu' sweet upon its thorny tree, And my false lover stole my rose, But, ah! he left the thorn wi' me.

# 80. THE WRAGGLE TAGGLE GIPSIES

English folk-song

1. Three—
2. They—

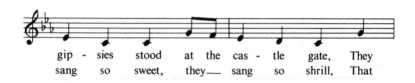

gip - sies stood at the cas - tle gate, They
sang so sweet, they— sang so shrill, That

sang so high, they— sang so low, The
fast her tears be - gan to flow, And

la - dy sate in her cham - ber late, Her
she laid down her— silk - en gown, Her

heart it melt - ed a - way as snow.
gold - en rings— and— all her show.

3    She pluck-ed off her high-heeled shoes,
       A-made of Spanish leather, O.
    She would in the street, with her bare, bare feet,
       All out in the wind and weather, O.

4    "O saddle to me my milk-white steed,
       And go and fetch me my pony, O.
    That I may ride and seek my bride,
       Who is gone with the wraggle taggle gipsies, O."

5    O he rode high, and he rode low,
       He rode through wood and copses too,
    Until he came to an open field,
       And there he espied his a-lady, O.

6    "What makes you leave your house and land,
       Your golden treasures for to go?
    What makes you leave your new-wedded lord,
       To follow the wraggle taggle gipsies, O?"

7    "What care I for my house and land?
       What care I for my treasure, O?
    What care I for my new-wedded lord?
       I'm off with the wraggle taggle gipsies, O!"

8    "Last night you slept on a goose-feather bed,
       With the sheet turned down so bravely, O.
    Tonight you'll sleep in a cold open field,
       Along with the wraggle taggle gipsies, O."

9    "What care I for a goose-feather bed,
       With the sheet turned down so bravely, O?
    Tonight I'll sleep in a cold open field,
       Along with the wraggle taggle gipsies, O."

# 81. WILL YE NO COME BACK AGAIN?

Scottish traditional tune, with words by Lady Nairne

1. Bon - nie Char - lie's noo a - wa,
2. Ye trust - ed in your Hie - land men, They

Safe - ly o'er the friend - ly main, Mony a heart will
trust - ed you, dear Char - lie; They kent your hid - ing

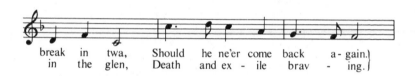

break in twa, Should he ne'er come back a - gain.⌉
in the glen, Death and ex - ile brav - ing.⌋

Will ye no come back a - gain? Will ye no come back a - gain?

Bet-ter loved ye can-na be, Will ye no come back a-gain?

3 Sweet's the laverock's note and lang,
  Lilting wildly up the glen;
 But aye to me he sings ae sang,
  "Will ye no come back again?"
   *Will ye no etc.*

# 82. WE BE THREE POOR MARINERS

English sea song, with tune and words from Ravenscroft's *Deuteromelia*, 1609

# 83. WALTZING MATILDA

Australian song, melody by Marie Cowan, words by A. B. Paterson

1. Once a jol-ly swag-man camped by a bil-la-bong,
2. Down came a jum-buck to drink at the bil-la-bong,

Un - der the shade of a cool - i - bah tree, And he
Up jumped the swag - man and grabbed him with glee, And he

sang as he watched and wait - ed till his bil - ly boiled,
sang as he stowed that jum-buck in his tuc-ker bag,

"You'll come a-waltz - ing Ma-til - da with me! Waltz-ing Ma- til - da,

waltz-ing Ma-til - da, You'll come a -waltz-ing Ma-til - da with me," (1.) And he
(2.) And he

sang as he watched and wait -ed till his bil - ly boiled,
sang as he stowed that jum-buck in his tuc-ker bag,

*"You'll come a - waltz - ing Ma - til - da with me."*

3    Up rode the squatter, mounted on his thoroughbred,
       Up rode the troopers, one, two, three:
    "Whose that jolly jumbuck you've got in your tuckerbag?
       *You'll come a-waltzing Matilda with me.*
    *Waltzing Matilda, waltzing Matilda,*
       *You'll come a-waltzing Matilda with me.*
    Whose that jolly jumbuck you've got in your tuckerbag?
       *You'll come a-waltzing Matilda with me!"*

4    Up jumped the swagman and sprang into the billabong,
       "You'll never take me alive," said he.
    And his ghost may be heard as you pass by that billabong:
       *"You'll come a-waltzing Matilda with me.*
    *Waltzing Matilda, waltzing Matilda,*
       *You'll come a-waltzing Matilda with me,"*
    And his ghost may be heard as you pass by that billabong:
       *" You'll come a-waltzing Matilda with me."*

swagman: a man on tramp carrying his swag, a bundle wrapped up in a blanket
billabong: a waterhole in the dried-up bed of a river
jumbuck: a sheep
squatter: a sheep-farmer on a large scale

# 84. THE VICAR OF BRAY

English 17th-century tune, with 18th-century words

1. In good King Charle-s's golden days, When loy-al-ty no harm meant, A zeal-ous high church-man was I, And so I got pre-fer-ment. To teach my flock I ne-ver missed, Kings were by God ap-point-ed, And lost are those that dare re-sist, Or touch the Lord's an-oint-ed.

2. When roy-al James poss-essed the crown, And Pop-ery came in fash-ion, The pe-nal laws I hoot-ed down, And read the Dec-lar-a-tion. The Church of Rome I found would fit Full well my con-sti-tu-tion, And I had been a Jes-u-it But for the Rev-o-lu-tion.

*And this is law I will main-tain Un-*

-til my— dy-ing— day, *Sir,* That what-so-ev-er king shall reign, I'll still be the Vi-car of Bray, *Sir.*

3    When William was our King declared
        To ease the nation's grievance,
    With this new wind about I steered
        And swore to him allegiance.
    Old principles I did revoke,
        Set conscience at a distance;
    Passive obedience was a joke,
        A jest was non-resistance.
          *And this is law etc.*

4    When royal Anne became our Queen,
        The Church of England's glory,
    Another face of things was seen
        And I became a Tory;
    Occasional conformists base,
        I blamed their moderation
    And thought the Church in danger was
        By such prevarication.
          *And this is law etc.*

5    Th' illustrious house of Hanover
        And Protestant succession,
    To them I do allegiance swear—
        While they can hold possession;
    For in my faith and loyalty
        I never more will falter,
    And George my lawful King shall be—
        Until the times do alter.
          *And this is law etc.*

# 85. SONG OF THE WESTERN MEN

Cornish traditional tune, with words by the Rev. R. S. Hawker. Trelawny, Bishop of Bristol, was one of the seven bishops imprisoned in the Tower of London by King James II.

1. A ___ good sword and a trust - y hand! A ___ mer - ry heart and true! King ___ Jame - s's men shall un - der - stand What ___ Corn - ish lads ___ can ___ do. And ___ have they fixed the where and when? And ___

2. Out ___ spake their cap - tain brave and bold, A ___ mer - ry wight was he: "If ___ Lon - don Tower were Mich - ael's ___ hold, We'll ___ set Tre - law - ny ___ free! We'll ___ cross the Ta - mar, land to land, The ___

3. "And ___ when we come to Lon - don Wall, A ___ pleas - ant sight to view, Come ___ forth, come forth, ye cow - ards ___ all, Here's ___ men as good ___ as ___ you! Tre - -law - ny, he's in keep and hold, Tre -

shall Tre - law - ny die? Here's_ twen - ty thou - sand
Sev - ern is no stay, With_ 'One and all,' and
-law - ny, he may die, But_ twen - ty thou - sand

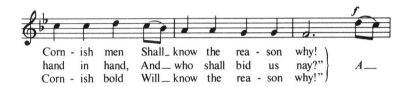

Corn - ish men Shall_ know the rea - son why!
hand in hand, And_ who shall bid us nay?"    A—
Corn - ish bold Will_ know the rea - son why!"

good sword and a trus - ty hand! A___

mer - ry heart and true! King_ Jame-s's men shall

un - der - stand What_ Corn - ish lads_ can_ do.

89

# 86. THE OAK AND THE ASH

English traditional song (tune c. 1650)

1. A north-country maid up to Lon-don had strayed, Al-though with her na-ture it did not a-gree; She wept and she sighed, and bit-ter-ly she cried, "I wish once a-gain in the north I could be.

2. "While sad-ly I roam I re-gret my dear home, Where lads and young lass-es are mak-ing the hay; The bells they do ring, and the birds they do sing, The fields and the gar-dens are plea-sant and gay.

3. "No doubt, did I please, I could mar-ry with ease; Where maid-ens are fair ma-ny lov-ers will come; But he whom I wed must be north-coun-try bred, And car-ry me back to my north-coun-try home.

Oh! the oak, and the ash, and the bon-ny i-vy tree, They flour-ish at home in my own coun-try."

# 87. MY BONNY CUCKOO

British folk-song

1. My bon - ny cuc - koo,___ I tell thee true That through___ the groves I'll___ rove with you: I'll rove with you un - til the next spring And then my cuc - koo shall___ sweet - ly sing. "Cuc - koo, Cuc - koo," un - til the next spring, And then my cuc - koo shall___ sweet - ly sing.

2. The ash and the haz - el shall sad - ly say, "My bon - ny cuc - koo, don't___ go a - way, Don't go a - way, but tar - ry here And make___ the sea - son___ last all the year. Cuc - koo, Cuc - koo, pray tar - ry here, And sing___ for us through - out the year."

# 88. THE MINSTREL BOY

Irish traditional tune, with words by Thomas Moore

**Moderato**

1. The min - strel boy to the war is gone, In the ranks of death you'll find him; His fa - ther's sword he has gird - ed on, And his wild harp slung be - hind him. "Land of song!" said the war - rior-bard, "Though all the world be - trays thee, *One* sword, at least, thy rights shall guard, *One* faith - ful harp shall praise thee."

2. The min - strel fell, but the foe - man's chain Could not bring his proud soul un - der; The harp he loved nev - er spoke a - gain, For he tore its chords a - sun - der, And said, "No chains shall sul - ly thee, Thou soul of love and brav - er - y! Thy songs were made for the pure and free, They shall nev - er sound in slav - 'ry."

92

# 89. THE MILLER OF DEE

English 17th-century tune, with 18th-century words

1. There was a jolly miller once Lived on the river Dee,___ He worked and sang from morn till night, No lark more blithe than he.___ And__ this the burden of his song For ever used to be,___ "I care for nobody, no, not I, If nobody cares for me.___

2. "I live by my mill, she is to me Like parent, child, and wife,___ I would not change my station For any other in life.___ No__ lawyer, surgeon, or doctor E'er had a groat from me,___ I care for nobody, no, not I, If nobody cares for me."___

3. Then like the miller, bold and free, Let us rejoice and sing,___ The days of youth were made for glee, And time is on the wing.___ The__ song shall pass from me to thee, And round this jovial ring,___ And all in heart__ and voice, agree To sing, "Long live the King."___

*D.C.*

93

# 90. THE MERMAID

English traditional song

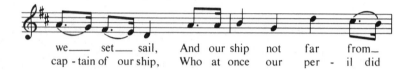

1. One— Fri - day morn when
2. And— then up spoke the

we— set— sail, And our ship not far from—
cap - tain of our ship, Who at once our per - il did

land, We— there did es - py— a—
see, "I have mar - ried a wife— in

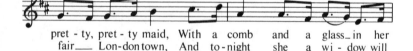

pret - ty, pret - ty maid, With a comb and a glass— in her
fair— Lon - don town, And to - night she a wi - dow will

hand, her hand, her hand, With a comb and a glass— in her
be, will be, will be, And to - night she a wi - dow will

hand.
be." } *While the ra - ging seas— did—*

**94**

roar, *And the stor - my winds did____*

blow, *And____ we jol - ly sai - lor boys were*

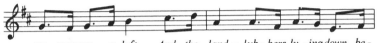

up, were up a-loft, *And the land - lub - bers ly - ing down be -*

*D.C.*

-low, be-low, be-low, *And the land - lub - bers ly - ing down be - low.*

3    And then up spoke the little cabin boy,
    And a fair-haired boy was he,

"I've a father and mother in fair Portsmouth town,

    And tonight they will weep for me, for me, for me,
    And tonight they will weep for me."

4    Then three times round went our gallant ship,
    And three times round went she,

Then three times round went our gallant, gallant ship
    And she sank to the bottom of the sea, the sea, the sea,
    And she sank to the bottom of the sea.

# 91. MEN OF HARLECH

Welsh traditional song, with words by Thomas Oliphant. The song refers to the siege of Harlech Castle (held by Dafydd ap Jevan) by the Earl of Pembroke in the reign of Edward IV.

**In march time**

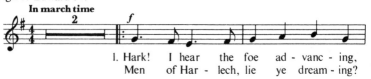

1. Hark! I hear the foe ad - vanc - ing,
Men of Har - lech, lie ye dream - ing?

Barb - èd steeds are proud - ly pranc - ing, Hel - mets, in the
See ye not their fal - chions gleam - ing? While their pen - nants

sun - beams glanc - ing, Glit - ter through the trees.
gai - ly stream - ing Flut - ter in the breeze.

From the rocks re - bound - ing, Let the war - cry

sound - ing Sum - mon all At Cam - bria's call, The

haugh - ty__ foe__ sur - round - ing. Men of Har - lech,

96

on to glo - ry! See, your_ ban - ner

famed in sto - ry Waves these burn - ing

words be - fore ye, "Brit- ain scorns to yield."

2    Mid the fray, see dead and dying,
Friend and foe together lying,
All around the arrows flying
    Scatter sudden death.
Frightened steeds are wildly neighing,
Brazen trumpets hoarsely braying,
Wounded men for mercy praying
    With their parting breath.
See they're in disorder!
Comrades, keep close order!
    Ever they
    Shall rue the day
They ventured o'er the border.
Now the Saxon flees before us,
Vict'ry's banner floateth o'er us,
Raise the loud exulting chorus,
    "Britain wins the field."

# 92. THE MALLOW FLING

British 18th-century tune, with words by A.H. Body

1. Now the sun is shin-ing bright-ly,__
2. Till the fires of night are burn-ing,__

Old and young and stiff and spright-ly,__
Dance they all, sad sor-row spurn-ing,__

Tread-ing swift-ly, tread-ing light-ly, Dance the Fling at
Hap-py then to home re-turn-ing From the Fling at

Mal - low.
Mal - low. Oh, the danc-ing through the town,

Oh, the pranc-ing up and down, Priest and par-son,

king and clown, Dance the Fling at Mal - low.

# 93. LOCH LOMOND

Scottish traditional song (words and melody attributed to Lady John Scott)

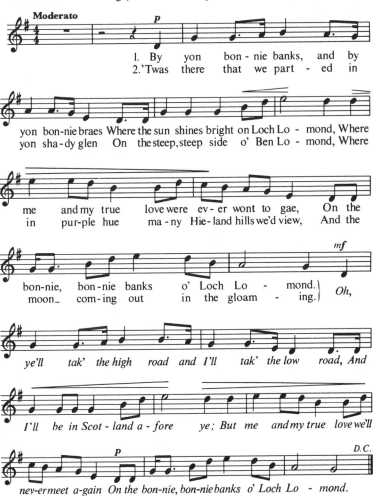

1. By yon bon-nie banks, and by yon bon-nie braes Where the sun shines bright on Loch Lo - mond, Where me and my true love were ev-er wont to gae, On the bon-nie, bon-nie banks o' Loch Lo - mond.

2. 'Twas there that we part-ed in yon sha-dy glen On the steep, steep side o' Ben Lo - mond, Where in pur-ple hue ma-ny Hie-land hills we'd view, And the moon_ com-ing out in the gloam - ing.

Oh, ye'll tak' the high road and I'll tak' the low road, And I'll be in Scot-land a-fore ye; But me and my true love we'll nev-er meet a-gain On the bon-nie, bon-nie banks o' Loch Lo - mond.

# 94. HIGH GERMANY

Somerset folk-song

1. O Pol - ly, love, O Pol - ly, the rout has now be - gun, And we must march a - way at the beat - ing of the drum: Go dress your - self in all your best and come a - long with me, I'll take you to the cru - el wars in High Ger - man - y.

2. O Har - ry, dear, O Har - ry, you mind what I do say, My feet they are so ten - der, I can - not march a - way, Be - sides, my dear - est Har - ry, though I'm in love with thee, How am I fit for cru - el wars in High Ger - man - y?

3. Oh, curs - ed were the cru - el wars that ev - er they should rise, And out of mer - ry Eng - land press many a lad like - wise! They pressed my Har - ry from me, like - wise my bro - thers three, And sent them to the cru - el wars in High Ger - man - y.

# 95. HEART OF OAK

Tune by William Boyce, with words by David Garrick.
The 'wonderful year' was 1759, the 'year of victories'.

1. Come, cheer up, my lads, 'tis to glo - ry we steer, To add some - thing more to this won - der - ful year; To\_ hon - our we call you, not press you like slaves, For who are so free as the sons of the waves? }

2. We ne'er see our foes but we wish them to stay, They ne - ver see us but they wish us a - way, If they run, why, we fol - low, and run them a - shore, For if they won't fight us, we can - not do more. }

*Heart of oak are our ships, Jol - ly tars are our men; We al - ways are rea - dy.*

*Stea - dy, boys, stea - dy, We'll fight\_and we'll con - quer a - gain and a - gain.*

# 96. THE FLIGHT OF THE EARLS

Irish traditional tune, with words by A. P. Graves

1. To o - ther shores a -cross the sea We speed with swell - ing sail; Yet still there lin - gers on our lee A phan-tom In - nis-fail. Oh, fear not, fear not, gen - tle ghost, Your sons shall turn un - true! Tho' fain to fly your love - ly coast, They leave their hearts with you.

2. As slow - ly in - to dist - ance dim Your sha - dow sinks and dies, So o'er the o - cean's ut - most rim An - oth - er realm shall rise. New hills shall swell, new vales ex-pand, New ri - vers wind - ing flow, But could we for a fos - ter land Your mo - ther love fore - go?

3. Shall migh - ty *Es - pan's mar - tial praise Our pa - triot pul - ses still, And o'er your mem-'ry's fer - vent rays For ev - er cast a chill? Oh no! we live for your re - lief, Till, home from a - lien earth, We share the smile that gilds your grief, The tear that gems your mirth.

\* Espan's = Spain's

# 97. DRINK TO ME ONLY

Tune by an unknown composer, c. 1770, to words by Ben Jonson

1. Drink to me on - ly with thine eyes, And
2. I sent thee late a ro - sy wreath, Not

I will pledge with mine, Or leave a kiss with-
so much hon' - ring thee As giv-ing it a

-in the cup And I'll not ask for wine; The
hope that there It could not with - ered be; But

thirst that from the soul doth rise Doth
thou there - on didst on - ly breathe, And

ask a drink di - vine, But might I of Jove's
sendst it back to me, Since when it grows, and

nec - tar sup I would not change for thine.
smells, I swear, Not of it - self, but thee.

# 98. DARBY KELLY

Tune by John Whitaker, with words adapted from Charles Dibdin

1. My grand - sire beat the drum com- plete, His name was Dar - by Kel - ly O! No lad so true__ at rat - tat - too, At roll - call or re - -veil - lez O! When Marl - bro's name first rose to fame, So

2. A son he had, who was my dad, The sec - ond Dar - by Kel - ly O! As quick and true__ at rat - tat - too, At roll - call or re - -veil - lez O! When great Wolfe died, his count- ry's pride, To

3. And now, small blame, I bear the name And drum of Dar - by Kel - ly O! My - self as true__ to rat - tat - too, To roll - call or re - -veil - lez O! With Wel - ling-ton, old Ire - land's son, I've

proud    he   roll'd_ the Point   of  War,_____    At
arms,    to   arms_ the fath - er beat,_____    Each
beat     the  Moun-seers out   of Spain, ____    And

Blen - heim he   and   Ra - mil - lies___ Fired
dale    and hill   re - mem - bers  still___ How
now    we march   through lau - rel  arch___ And

all    our cham - pions to   the core,  And Oh,  his wrist had
loud   and long, how clear  and sweet!  And when for home from
wav - ing ban - ners home  a - gain;  And as  my sticks the

such    a   twist,   When  home    they march'd_ with
off     the  foam    He    led     the  march___ with
same    old tricks   They  play    with  patt - 'ring

row - dow - dow,_____    With  one  great shout the
row - dow - dow,_____    Och!  what  a   shout the
row - dow - dow, _____   Man,  wo - man, child, they've

boys  came out,_ The girls    they gazed, you don't  know how!
lads  let  out,_ The las - ses looked, you don't  know how!
all   gone wild,_ The girls    they gaze,  you don't  know how!

# 99. BONNIE DUNDEE

Scottish traditional tune, with words by Sir Walter Scott

1. To the Lords of Con-ven-tion 'twas
2. Dun - dee he is moun-ted, he

Clav'r-house who spoke: "Ere the King's crown shall fall there are
rides up the street, The— bells are rung back-ward, the

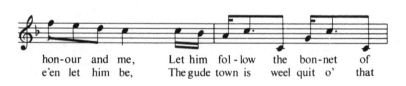

crowns to be broke, Then— each cav-a-lier who loves
drums they are beat, But the Pro-vost, douce man, said, "Just

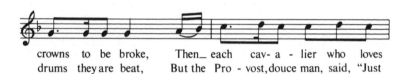

hon-our and me, Let him fol-low the bon-net of
e'en let him be, The gude town is weel quit o' that

Bon-nie Dun-dee."⎫
De'il o' Dun-dee."⎭   *Come fill up my cup,— come*

*fill  up  my  can,      Come  sad - dle  your  hor - ses,  and*

*call  out  your  men,      Come  op - en  the  West  Port,  and*

*let me gang free,   And it's room for    the bon-nets  of  Bon-nie  Dun-dee.*

3    There are hills beyond Pentland, and lands beyond Forth,
     Be there lords in the Lowlands, they've chiefs in the North;
     There are wild Du-nie-was-sals, three thousand times three,
     Will cry "Hoi" for the bonnet of Bonnie Dundee.
          *Come fill up my cup etc.*

4    "Then away to the hills, to the caves, to the rocks—
     Ere I own a usurper, I'll crouch with the fox;
     And tremble, false Whigs, in the midst of your glee,
     You have not seen the last of my bonnet and me."
          *Come fill up my cup etc.*

# 100. THE BAY OF BISCAY

Tune by John Davy, with words by Andrew Cherry

1. Loud roars the dread-ful thun - der, The__ rain a de - luge__ show'rs,
2. Now dashed up - on the bil - low, Our__ op - 'ning tim - bers__ creak,

The__ clouds were rent a - sun - der By__ light - ning's vi - vid__
Each__ fears a wa - t'ry pil - low, None__ stops the dread - ful__

pow'rs; The__ night was drear and
leak. To__ cling to slip - p'ry

dark,     Our   poor    de - vo - ted__   bark__
shrouds    Each   breath - less   sea - man_   crowds,__

Till    next_   day,     there   she_   lay,     In _ the_
As    she _   lay,     till   the_   day,     In _ the_

*D.C.*

**1**      **2**

Bay_ of_ Bis - cay,    O!       O!
Bay_ of_ Bis - cay,    O!       O!

3    At length the wished-for morrow
       Breaks through the hazy sky,
    Absorbed in silent sorrow
       Each heaved a bitter sigh.
    The dismal wreck to view
    Struck horror to the crew,
    As she lay, on that day,
    In the Bay of Biscay, O!

4    Her yielding timbers sever,
       Her pitchy seams are rent,
    When Heav'n, all-bounteous ever,
       Its boundless mercy sent.
    A sail in sight appears,
    We hail her with three cheers.
    Now we sail, with the gale,
    From the Bay of Biscay, O!

# ACKNOWLEDGMENTS

Thanks are due as follows for permission to reprint words and melodies:

Allans Music (Australia) Pty. Ltd.—(*words and melody*): Waltzing Matilda.

American Folklore Society Inc.—(*words and melody*): Scraping up Sand.

E. J. Arnold & Son Ltd. —(*words and melody*): Green and White.

C. C. Birchard & Co.—(*words*): The Cobbler and the Crow.

Boosey & Hawkes Ltd.—(*words*): The Flight of the Earls (from the *New National Song Book*).

Co-operative Recreation Service Inc.—(*words and melody*): The Cuckoo.

J. Curwen & Sons Ltd.—(*words and melodies*): This Old Man, Boney was a Warrior, Blow away the Morning Dew, The Wraggle Taggle Gipsies.

E. P. Dutton & Co. Inc.—(*words and melody*): Sacramento (collected by Stan Hugill).

Mrs. MacMahon and University of London Press—(*words and melody*): The Fox's Song.

Thomas Nelson & Sons Ltd.—(*words*): What shall we do with the Drunken Sailor? (2 verses), The Mallow Fling.

Novello & Co. Ltd.—(*words*): The Gay Musician, (*melody*): Elsie Marley, (*words and melodies*): There was a Jolly Miller, The Keeper, The Farmyard, John Barleycorn, The Tree in the Wood (collected by Cecil Sharp), High Germany (collected by H. E. D. Hammond).

Oxford University Press—(*words*): The Riddle, Andulko, Ho-la-hi, Captain Morgan's March (from Oxford School Music Books); The Smuggler's Song (from Clarendon Class Singing Course); Fisherman's Night Song; Spring Song (from Sixty Songs for Little Children); Punchinello, The Merry Cobbler (from A Second Sixty Songs); Anna Marie, Come Home Now (from A Third Sixty Songs); The Shepherdess (from the Clarendon Song Books); (*words and melodies*): Donkey Riding, Rio Grande, What shall we do with the Drunken Sailor? (from the Oxford Song Books).

The Peacock Collection, National Museum of Canada—(*words and melody*): I'se the B'y.

Routledge & Kegan Paul Ltd.—(*words and melody*): Sacramento (collected by Stan Hugill).

Frederick Ungar Publishing Co.—(*words and melody*): Jim along Josie (from The American Play-Party Song by B. A. Botkin, © 1937, 1963 by B. A. Botkin).